CONTEMPORARY'S

ATTRACTIONS

BOOK THREE

SUN AND GAMES

ETHEL TIERSKY
MAXINE CHERNOFF

CB

CONTEMPORARY
BOOKS

CHICAGO

Library of Congress Cataloging-in-Publication Data

Tiersky, Ethel, 1937-
    Sun and games / Ethel Tiersky.
       p.   cm. — (Attractions ; bk. 3)
    ISBN 0-8092-3686-9
    1. Readers—United States.   2. English language—Textbooks for
foreign speakers.   3. Resorts—United States—Problems,
exercises, etc. I. Title. II. Series: Tiersky, Ethel, 1937-
Attractions ; bk. 3.
PE1127.H5T46   1993
428.6′4—dc20   93-47562
                                        CIP

Acknowledgments

We wish to thank the following for sending us background information, answering innumerable questions by phone, and, in some cases, supplying photographs for this text.

"Neon Oasis": Ken Evans, Media Relations Manager, Public Relations Department, Nevada Commission on Tourism, Carson City, Nevada; Kimberly Graham, Vice President, Fleishman-Hillard, Inc., Los Angeles, California.

"Elvis's Kingdom": Karyn Jakubszak, Administrative Assistant, Communications Department, Graceland, Division of Elvis Presley Enterprises, Inc., Memphis, Tennessee.

"Enchanted Land": John Chaney, Tanner Chaney Gallery, Albuquerque, New Mexico; Debra Owen, Administrative Coordinator, Sandia Peak Tram Company, Albuquerque, New Mexico; Patty Taylor, Public Relations Coordinator, Taos County Chamber of Commerce, Taos, New Mexico.

"Winter Wonderland": Jane Schrandt, Public Relations Department, Mall of America, Bloomington, Minnesota.

Photo Credits

Cover photos: Las Vegas © Jake Rajs/The Image Bank, surfer in Hawaii © Don King/The Image Bank, hot air balloon © Allan Becker/The Image Bank; Pat Barrett: 35; Jay Blackwood: 38; Donna Caroll: 62, 66; Bob Firth: 76, 79, 81, 84; Graceland, Division of Elvis Presley Enterprises, Inc.: 16, 19, 24, 25, 26; © Alan Becker/The Image Bank: 32; Ami Koenig: 2, 4; Don Laine: 41; The Las Vegas News Bureau: 9; Luxor Las Vegas: 7; Tribune File Photos: 57, 71; UPI/Bettmann: 11, 46, 48, 54

Published by Contemporary Books, Inc.
Two Prudential Plaza, Chicago, Illinois 60601-6790
Manufactured in the United States of America
International Standard Book Number: 0-8092-3686-9
10 9 8 7 6 5 4 3 2

Published simultaneously in Canada by
Fitzhenry & Whiteside
195 Allstate Parkway
Markham, Ontario L3R 4T8
Canada

CONTENTS

TO THE READER

How many major hit singles did Elvis have during his career? Which islands are actually the crests of an underwater mountain range? Which Hollywood tradition began when a famous star stepped in the wrong place? These are just a few of the amazing facts you will discover in *Sun and Games*, the third book in the four-book reading series **Attractions**.

Attractions takes you to some of our nation's most visited sites. Each book contains six stories about famous places, things, and people—and the interesting facts behind them. Along the way, you will be able to check your understanding of what you have read. Each story closes with little-known tidbits about the city and state where the attraction is located.

- *Book One, It's Colossal*, features America's giant points of interest: the Statue of Liberty, Sears Tower, the Gateway Arch, Mount Rushmore, the Grand Canyon, and Walt Disney World.

- *Book Two, Back to the Past*, features sites that have important connections to our nation's past: Plimoth Plantation, the White House, New Orleans, the San Francisco Bay Area, the Vietnam Veterans Memorial, and the commonwealth of Puerto Rico.

- *Book Three, Sun and Games*, features the attractions of six of the country's most popular vacation spots: Las Vegas, Graceland, New Mexico, Hawaii, Hollywood, and Minnesota.

- *Book Four, Birthplaces of Ideas*, features places where some of our nation's most important social ideas and inventions began: philosopher Henry David Thoreau's Walden Pond, aviators Orville and Wilbur Wright's Kitty Hawk, inventor Thomas Edison's New Jersey, civil rights leader Martin Luther King Jr.'s Center for Nonviolent Social Change, architect Frank Lloyd Wright's Taliesin, and conservationist Rachel Carson's Greater Washington, D.C.

The stories in **Attractions** will inform you, entertain you, surprise you, and perhaps even shock you. At the same time, you will be building your knowledge about the geography of the United States.

The map below shows the locations of the sites featured in each of the four books. Those contained in *Sun and Games* are highlighted in blue.

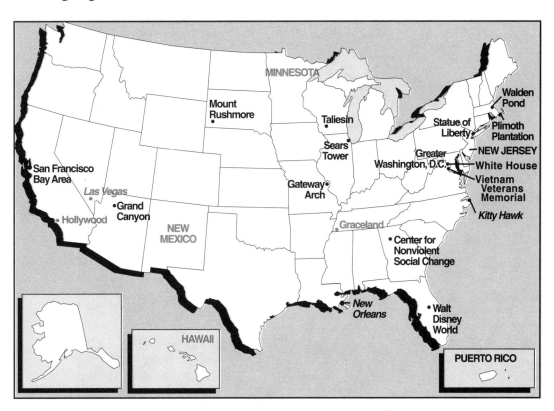

Once you've read the stories in *Sun and Games*, we invite you to explore the other three books in the **Attractions** series. As you do, you'll learn the stories behind some of the most famous places in America.

Vegas Vic welcomes you to downtown Las Vegas.

NEON OASIS

*This city in a desert attracts more tourists
than any other place in the United States. What city is it?
To find out, read on. . . .*

A High-Stakes Gamble

1   In 1946, a gangster opened a luxury hotel in the dusty gambling town of Las Vegas, Nevada. Most of the money to build it was borrowed from friends. Many were gangsters. Construction costs went millions of dollars over budget. When the fabulous Flamingo Hotel finally opened, business was slow. The casino lost money. Losing millions made the investors unhappy. So Benjamin "Bugsy" Siegel, big-shot gangster, was shot to death.

2   It was a painful ending for Bugsy but a neon-bright beginning for Las Vegas. Bugsy's murder was widely publicized. Curious people thronged[1] to see the fancy hotel that he had built. High rollers came in search of Lady Luck. Soon, the Flamingo was making a lot of money. More investors wanted a piece of the action. Nevada seemed the perfect place for a gambling center. In this state only, nearly every kind of gambling was and still is legal.

3   Eventually, gangsters were barred from investing in Las Vegas gambling casinos. Honest businesspeople came

---

[1]came in great numbers

in. The most famous was billionaire Howard Hughes. By the early 1970s, he was one of the richest men in the world because of his holdings in Las Vegas real estate.

4   Today, Nevada attracts 30 million visitors each year. When they arrive, 22 million head straight for Las Vegas. That's more than go to Orlando, Florida, the site of Walt Disney World.

5   What lures all these visitors? Large, lavish casinos. Many kinds of theme hotels. Good food and entertainment at reasonable prices. A quick marriage or divorce. A business convention. A family vacation that's exciting for adults and for kids. All these combine to pull in the crowds.

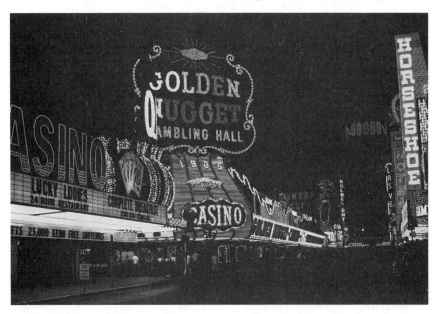

Las Vegas casinos

Checking Comprehension

What was Bugsy Siegel's role in the development of Las Vegas?

Besides the desire to gamble, what brings tourists to Las Vegas?

6   Driving or flying into Las Vegas after dark, newcomers may think they're seeing a mirage.[2] There's nothing but blackness in every direction. Then, suddenly, an oasis[3] of colorful neon signs lights up the sky.

7   The name Las Vegas means "the meadows" in Spanish. The city's nicknames suit it better: Entertainment Capital of the World, City of Lights, Monte Carlo of the West, City of Little Wedding Churches, and Sin City.

8   Surrounded by mountains, Las Vegas stands on a desert plain about 2,000 feet above sea level. It's located at the meeting place of three deserts (the Mojave [Mo·ha'vee], the Sonoran, and the Great Basin). Rarely does it rain in this desert city. Las Vegas averages 320 days of sunshine a year. Annual rainfall is about 4.2 inches. Average humidity is 20 percent. These figures are the lowest of all U.S. urban areas.

9   In the summer, daytime temperatures often reach 110° F in the shade. As a result, spring and fall are the busiest tourist seasons. During that period, daytime temperatures are in the pleasant 70s. Winter temperatures range in the 50s or 60s. Visitors see snow-capped mountains in the distance. Any time of year, high winds may blow into town. They sometimes shift all the sand from the west side of the city to the east.

Checking Comprehension

Why are the city's nicknames fitting?

What are the worst features of Las Vegas weather? What are the best?

---

[2]something that looks real but isn't
[3]a place providing enjoyable change from the surroundings

10 The Strip is a 3½-mile stretch of Las Vegas Boulevard. It has the world's most lavish hotels. Visitors expect restaurants, a swimming pool, a gambling casino, a health spa, nightclubs, and shops. But many hotels offer much more. For example:

- Circus Circus has a free three-ring circus, complete with a high-wire act. Next door to it is the $75 million, 5-acre Grand Slam Canyon waterpark.
- Caesar's Palace is a miniature re-creation of ancient Rome. Visitors can enjoy a Roman feast served by goddesses dressed in togas.[4]
- Excalibur takes guests back to the Middle Ages. Here, they can dine in the company of jousting[5] knights.
- Mirage is a $650 million hotel with a South Seas theme. In front is a huge waterfall and the famous erupting volcano. Mirage also has a tropical rain forest under a glass dome. In the hotel's "Beyond Belief" show, rare white tigers serve as a warning that gamblers must pay their debts.

11 The 1993–1994 additions to the Strip are just as lavish:

- Luxor's decor is done in ancient Egyptian style. The hotel complex is a 30-story pyramid. Sights include models of King Tut's tomb, Nile River boats, and a huge model of Egypt's Great Sphinx.[6]

---

[4]loose-fitting robes worn by ancient Romans
[5]fighting on horseback with swords
[6]a giant ancient rock sculpture with the head of an Egyptian monarch

Luxor Las Vegas Hotel

- Treasure Island is a pirate village. Hourly battles between pirates and sailors take place on Buccaneer[7] Bay.
- MGM-Grand is the world's largest hotel (5,014 rooms). Visitors enter the casino by walking through the paws of an 88-foot-tall MGM lion. Inside, there's a 33-acre Hollywood theme park with rides and shows. Total cost to build the MGM-Grand: $1 billion!

12   Tourists come to Las Vegas expecting to see big-name stars and extravagant shows. Several hotels have nightclubs that can seat 10,000 people. Las Vegas shows often include a chorus line of showgirls in skimpy costumes and feathered hats.

Checking Comprehension

Why are the hotels on the Strip unusual?
What types of shows are typical in Las Vegas?

---

[7]pirate

13   After dark is the best time to head downtown to Fremont Street. There, hotels and casinos compete for tourist attention. Tourists can see $1 million on display (in $10,000 bills) at Binion's Horseshoe Casino. They can also place a $1 million bet on a single roll of the dice or deal of the cards. Many patrons gamble downtown rather than on the Strip because Fremont Street casinos accept smaller bets.

14   After leaving the casinos, some tourists still have a few dollars. They may head for the Forum Shops at Caesar's. It's one of the world's most entertaining malls. The decor includes immense columns and arches, fountains, and statues. The statues talk, the fountains dance, and the sky goes from dawn to dusk in three hours. In addition, the shops sell clothing from all over the world.

15   Experts say that, in the long run, less than 1 person in 100 wins money from gambling. It's easy to see why. Las Vegas gambling is honest, but it certainly isn't fair. The house has an advantage. For example, when playing roulette, a bet on red pays even money—$5 from the house for each $5 spent—if red comes up. But there's less than a 50 percent chance that red will come up. The bettor loses if the ball lands in a black slot or in a 0 or 00 slot. Las Vegas casinos pull in gaming revenues of about $3 billion annually ($8 million daily).

16   What can you bet on in Las Vegas? Just about anything, including sporting events. Some casino games use wheels, such as Wheel of Fortune. Card games include blackjack, poker, and baccarat [ba·kuh·rah']. Craps is played with dice and offers many possible bets. Bingo and keno involve matching numbers. But slot machines are the most popular casino games. Winners can take home up to $6 million. On average, though, the house keeps 76 percent of the money thrown into slot machines. For table games,

Las Vegas casino gamblers

the house keeps about 30 percent. In recent years, video poker and video blackjack have become great favorites.

17   Casinos do all they can to get visitors to play and keep them playing. Many casinos stay open 24 hours a day. If visitors don't know the games, the casino offers classes. Regular customers may get credit if they are short of cash. If customers are thirsty, cocktail waitresses bring free drinks to the gaming tables. Players never know whether the hour is getting late. Most casinos have no clocks or windows. Casinos do not allow tourists to take photos inside the casino for fear they'll make gamblers nervous. But the casino has video cameras on the ceiling, watching everyone.

18   Who can play? Anyone 21 years old or older is welcome to play. Minors aren't even allowed to watch. But they can walk through the casinos. Which games offer the best chance of winning? That depends upon the kinds of bets placed. But many say blackjack gives experienced players the best odds.

Checking Comprehension

Why do the casinos always make a profit?
What do casinos do to keep people gambling?

Las Vegas—Then and Now

19 People have lived in the Las Vegas valley since 11,000 B.C. The earliest residents were hunters and basket-makers. By A.D. 800, Native Americans called Anasazi [Ah·nu·sah'zee] settled there. Later, wandering Indian tribes roamed southern Nevada.

20 In the 1840s, Spanish and Mexican caravans[8] traveled the Old Spanish trail from Santa Fe, New Mexico, to California. They stopped at Las Vegas Springs, a real oasis. An American explorer, John Frémont, came through in 1844. Vegas's main street downtown is named for him. In 1905, Las Vegas became the connecting spot for trains to and from Nevada mining towns.

21 During the Great Depression, 5,000 workers were employed building the immense Hoover Dam. The dam is located about 25 miles from Las Vegas, along the Arizona-Nevada border. When it was built, it was the tallest concrete dam in the world. It is still one of the tallest. Workers removed nine million tons of rock from Black Canyon and created a dam 726 feet tall and 1,244 feet long. Today, visitors can go down into the dam by elevator, but not all the way to the bottom. In 75 seconds, they zoom down about 44 floors and still don't reach the base. The dam's base (660 feet thick) contains enough concrete to pave a highway from New York to San Francisco.

22 Hoover Dam is very important. It supplies water and electric power to much of the Pacific southwest. It also keeps the Colorado River from flooding. Construction of the dam began during the presidency of Herbert Hoover, and it is named for him.

---

[8]groups traveling together on a long journey

The Colorado River pours over the Hoover Dam at the rate of 42,000 cubic feet per second.

23   Hoover Dam's reservoir[9] [rez'ur·vwahr], Lake Mead, is the largest man-made lake in the United States. It is a vacationer's dream for fishing, swimming, boating, and other water sports. Lake Mead's water irrigates farmland in Arizona, Nevada, and southern California. In addition, the lake provides water for consumption in these states.

24   In 1935, when the dam was finished, many workers stayed on. Nevada legalized gambling in 1931. By the mid-1930s, Fremont Street had several casinos. Since the late 1940s, fancy hotels have been springing up along the Strip.

25   Las Vegas is one of the nation's most rapidly growing urban areas. Many people move to Las Vegas after retiring. A well-known retirement development just northwest of the city is called Sun City–Summerlin.

---

[9]a place for storing large amounts of water

26   Every year, nearly 75,000 marriages are performed in Las Vegas. Why? In Nevada, there's no waiting period and no blood test needed. Minimum age is 18. With parental consent, 16- or 17-year-olds can also marry. Dozens of chapels offer no-frills weddings. Some also offer a ceremony with a rented bridal gown, organ music, and flowers. On weekends, couples line up outside chapels awaiting their 15-minute weddings. Others get married in front of the Mirage Hotel just as the volcano erupts.

27   Nevada is also a popular place for getting a divorce. In 1931, the state cut the residency requirement[10] from six months to three months. Because of this, Nevada has become known as the nation's divorce capital.

28   In recent years, Las Vegas tourism has enjoyed another periodic boom. The tourist population has been growing by a million people a year. Las Vegas is no longer just a place for gambling in luxury. It has water sports, golf, horseback riding, museums, and 750 restaurants. It's a vacation spot for everyone.

Checking Comprehension

How did the Hoover Dam help Las Vegas develop?
Why does Las Vegas attract nongambling tourists?

---

[10]the length of time a person must live in a particular place to have certain legal rights there

SIDELIGHTS

About Las Vegas

- Visitors spend $10 billion a year.
- It has the world's 10 largest hotels.
- It has a total of 80,000 hotel rooms.
- About 63 percent of southern Nevada's workforce is employed by the tourist industry.
- The city's population is over 300,000; the county's, more than 850,000.
- About 3,500 people a month move to Las Vegas.

About Nevada, the Silver State

- Nevada mines about two-thirds of the country's gold, and it leads all states in silver production.
- The federal government owns 85 percent of Nevada's land—more than in any other state except Alaska.
- Nevada is the driest of the 50 states. Its average annual rainfall is 9 inches.
- Nevada's highest recorded temperature is 122° F; its lowest is −50° F.
- The oldest tree was discovered on Mount Wheeler in Nevada. It was 5,100 years old.
- Lake Tahoe, on the Nevada-California border, is one of the deepest lakes in the country. Its greatest depth is 1,640 feet. This beautiful glacial lake is popular for water sports and fishing.

Making Inferences

Reread the paragraph(s) indicated after each statement. Then decide if each statement is probably true or false.

_____ 1. The gangsters who invested in the Flamingo probably murdered Bugsy Siegel. (paragraph 1)

_____ 2. There are no big cities near Las Vegas. (paragraph 6)

_____ 3. Las Vegas is built on low, flat, dry land. (paragraph 8)

_____ 4. Outdoor tennis is very popular in Las Vegas during the summer. (paragraph 9)

_____ 5. The Mirage Hotel has real white tigers. (paragraph 10)

_____ 6. Las Vegas casinos have no clocks so that gamblers will forget the time. (paragraph 17)

_____ 7. Las Vegas is the only city in Nevada that makes marriage and divorce very quick and easy. (paragraphs 25–26)

Practicing Vocabulary

Circle the correct word or phrase to complete each sentence.

1. The money that a business or industry takes in is called (revue, revenue, skimpy, profits).
2. Las Vegas is (a barge, an oasis, a toga, a mirage).
3. When scientists dig underground for very old things, they are looking for (modern, unusual, everyday, ancient) artifacts.
4. (An erupting, A video, An extravagant, A broken) slot machine allows poker players to make some decisions about the hands they are playing.
5. Jousting knights are (fighting, dancing, gambling, drinking).

6. People lost in the desert imagine they see an oasis. But there's no water there. It's a (volcano, mirage, tomb, barge).
7. People come to Las Vegas to gamble in (caravans, casinos, barges, reservoirs).

Talking It Over

1. Do you consider gambling a harmless form of entertainment or a great social evil? Are you for or against increasing legal betting to help state governments raise money?
2. Gamblers Anonymous now has 600 chapters nationwide. Why do you think a person becomes a compulsive gambler? Could it ever happen to you? Why or why not?
3. Would you like to vacation in Las Vegas? If so, how long would you stay?
4. William Ramsey and M. W. Travers discovered neon gas in 1898. In 1895, Charles Fey invented the Liberty Bell, the first slot machine. In your opinion, which has done more for Vegas—the neon sign or the slot machine? Why?

Elvis Presley performing in the 1950s

ELVIS'S KINGDOM

How many major hit singles did Elvis have during his career? To find out, read on. . . .

Long Live the King!

1 It's January 8. In front of a Memphis, Tennessee, mansion, hundreds of people are sharing a birthday cake. They are remembering the birth of their favorite rock star, who died in 1977.

2 Gone but not forgotten—that phrase certainly applies to Elvis Presley. Fans continue to buy records, souvenirs, and other products bearing his name. They also pay to tour his home. His estate earns about $15 million a year from these sources.

3 Elvis's popularity can be measured in love as well as money. In 1992, about 670,000 visitors toured Graceland, his home. It has become the nation's most visited home after the White House. Tourists often ask, "How much is Elvis's home worth?" One guide has a quick answer, "It's priceless. Just like him."

4 The former king of rock 'n' roll is buried in the Meditation Garden near his mansion. On the anniversary of his death, August 16, thousands of tearful fans flock to Graceland. They carry candles in a moonlight walk to the burial

site. More people come to visit Elvis's grave than President John Kennedy's.

5   The week that marks the anniversary of Elvis's death now is called Elvis Week or International Tribute Week. Memphis hosts concerts and other events for the occasion. Some of the admission fees go to charity.

6   Elvis's fame is evident in other ways. He's the subject of about 150 songs, 160 books, and 300 college courses. At least 25 people (including one woman) earn their full-time livings impersonating[1] Elvis. Hundreds more perform part-time as Elvis look-alikes. All of this helps to keep Elvis's memory alive.

Checking Comprehension

What facts prove that Elvis Presley hasn't been forgotten?
What happens at Graceland on the anniversaries of his
        birth and death?

From Rags to Riches

7   Elvis was born in 1935. His birthplace in Tupelo, Mississippi, is now a state historic landmark. It is open to the public. Elvis's father built the little wooden cabin for $180. It had no indoor plumbing. Even after it had been wired for electricity, the Presleys used oil lamps. They had no money to pay electric bills.

8   When Elvis was 13, the family moved to Memphis, Tennessee. Poverty followed them there. Still, young Elvis owned a guitar. His mother bought it as a birthday present, instead of the gun her son had asked for. There were other musical influences: The church introduced him to gospel

---

[1]performing like another person

18

music. Memphis was the home of the blues. Nashville was the heart of country music. Later, Elvis combined all these styles with rock 'n' roll and created *rockabilly*.

9 At the age of 18, Elvis was a truck driver earning $41 a week. That year, 1953, he paid $4 to Sam Phillips, head of Sun Records, to cut his first record in a studio. He recorded the song "My Happiness" as a birthday gift to his mother. A year later, he sang on "The Grand Ole Opry," a famous Nashville radio show. It was broadcast before a live audience. Many country and western singers improved their careers after appearing on this show. But Elvis was a flop. The "Opry" manager told him to go back to truck driving. Elvis cried all the way home.

10 Then, in 1956, Elvis's career took off. He had six records that sold more than a million copies. He also appeared on a popular TV variety show, "The Milton Berle Show."

The Hall of Gold Records in Graceland displays Elvis's gold records.

Elvis had a good, but not a great, voice and only limited skills on the guitar. So what was all the fuss about? He was handsome, energetic, and different. He didn't just stand in front of a microphone and sing. He shook his legs and twisted his hips to the music. The motions earned him the name Elvis the Pelvis. Many adults didn't like his long sideburns, his defiant[2] expression, his tight pants, and his wild style. Parents of teenage girls thought of Elvis as Evil Presley. But the teenagers themselves loved him.

11   Later in 1956, Elvis performed on three Ed Sullivan TV variety shows. By the third show, Elvis was shown only from the waist up. Next came a movie contract—three films for $450,000. Elvis was on his way to becoming world famous. He was then only 21 years old. The following year, he bought Graceland, a mansion on 13.8 acres of land. He paid $100,000 in cash for it. For the rest of his life, Graceland was his home.

12   Elvis was the first important rock soloist. His early hits combined the ingredients now called rock 'n' roll. It blended African-American, country, and western music. The songs had a strong rhythmic beat. They were accompanied by the electric guitar. Elvis didn't invent this type of music, but his success spread rock music worldwide.

Checking Comprehension

How did Elvis's birthplace compare to Graceland?
Why was Tennessee a good place for Elvis to grow up?
What are some of the ingredients of rock music?

---

[2]resistant to authority

13 After serving in the army from 1958 to 1960, Elvis returned to Hollywood. His film career included 33 movies. None of them were very good, but they made money. Elvis asked his manager, Colonel Tom Parker, to get him better scripts. He wanted to develop his acting. But his manager was satisfied with financial success. Elvis didn't like being a movie star. He missed working before live audiences.

14 Parker controlled Elvis's career and his personal life. Once, President Richard Nixon invited Elvis to sing at the White House. Parker asked for a $25,000 fee. He was told that the White House never paid performers. Parker replied that Elvis never performed for free. So Elvis missed the great honor of performing at the White House.

15 In 1970, Elvis went to the White House for another reason. He went to offer President Nixon his help in the nation's fight against drug abuse. Nixon and Elvis were photographed together. Today, fans buy T-shirts with that photo and the caption "The President and the King."

16 Elvis feared that marriage would hurt his career. But Colonel Parker wanted Elvis to settle down. So, in 1967, Elvis married his girlfriend, Priscilla Beaulieu [Bu·loo']. She became the mother of his only child, Lisa Marie.

17 Like most entertainers, Elvis became a product packaged to appeal to the public. He dyed his brown hair black to look more dramatic. He copied the James Dean sneer because he thought girls liked that look. Elvis claimed that

his movements were caused by nervousness and a natural response to the music. But Elvis also knew that his audiences came to look as well as listen. His movements were part of the show. So were his fancy costumes. These included a $10,000 gold lamé [la·may']³ suit.

Checking Comprehension

What was Colonel Parker's main concern?
Why might Elvis have thought that marriage would hurt his career?

A Downhill Slide

18   Priscilla left Elvis in 1972. The breakup of his marriage was very painful for him. His weight increased, and his energy decreased. He continued to have a few gold records a year and do some live performances. In 1973, his TV special was broadcast internationally by satellite from Hawaii. It was a huge success. But Elvis was harming his health. He took a lot of prescription drugs. Some were to decrease his appetite. Others were to help him sleep all day or stay awake all night. (He preferred the night.) Graceland became a hideout. There, Elvis spent several days at a time just lying in bed.

19   Elvis's lifetime earnings may have reached $18 billion. He could buy anything he wanted, and he usually did. He enjoyed surprising friends and fans with unexpected gifts. One day, he noticed a woman admiring his car, which was parked in front of an automobile dealer. He told her, "You can't have that. It's mine. But I'll buy you another. Go into the showroom, and pick the one you like." She did, and Elvis paid the bill.

---

³fabric made with metallic threads, often gold or silver

20   He enjoyed the luxuries his wealth could buy. Still, in the spring of 1977, he told a friend, "I'm sort of getting tired of being Elvis Presley." That same spring, he gave his last concert. He looked overweight in his jumpsuit. Sweat poured down his face. He didn't have the energy to move much. He forgot the words to songs he had been singing for years. But his loyal audience cheered him.

21   A few months later, Elvis was found dead on the bathroom floor at Graceland. He was only 42 years old. The official report said that he died of a heart attack.

22   Years later, a sense of mystery about Elvis's death remains. Some think he was murdered. Some fans still refuse to believe that he's dead. They say that he faked his death and is living in hiding. Elvis sightings continue to be news. What really happened to Elvis? According to his ex-wife, he was ruined by too much wealth before he was mature enough to handle it. He was also the victim of people who gave him everything he wanted. He was a self-made man who self-destructed.

Checking Comprehension

Do you think Elvis enjoyed his life? Discuss what was
    good and bad about it.
Why might Elvis have been unhappy?
What killed Elvis?

---

23   Visitors to Graceland come up Elvis Presley Boulevard to the Music Gate. It is decorated with musical notes and guitarists. This tall iron gate was one of Elvis's early additions to his home. It protected him from excited fans, who were always around when he was at home. Sometimes Elvis came by with gifts for them. Sometimes he watched the activity at the gate from closed-circuit TV in his bedroom. During his 20 years at Graceland, the Music Gate needed frequent repairs.

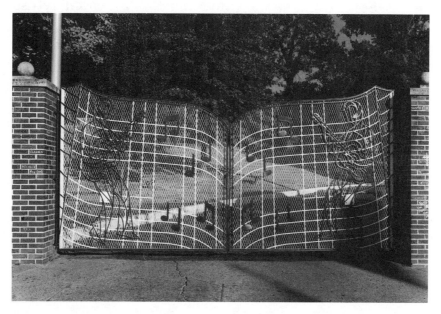

The Music Gate at the entrance of Graceland

24   The exterior of Graceland, with its white pillars, looks like a typical Southern mansion. Inside, the mansion's 23 rooms are decorated in Elvis's lavish taste. Visitors notice Elvis's fondness for blue with gold trim, black with deep pink, and red with more red. He also liked chandeliers, mirrors, deep carpets, and velvet fabrics. He had at least one TV set in every room.

Elvis's Graceland mansion

25   In some rooms, the decor[4] gets really wild. The Jungle Room is done in South Pacific style. The Pool Room has a pool table in an 1890s setting. The den has a carpeted ceiling and a full-wall waterfall.

26   The Trophy Room holds Elvis's awards. It's quite a collection. Elvis was the most successful solo recording artist of all time. He earned 56 gold and platinum awards. He had 170 major hit singles and more than 80 top-selling albums from 1956 through 1977.

27   Outside, there's a swimming pool that Elvis, a non-swimmer, had installed. There's also a racquetball court, which he did use. In the Meditation Garden, Elvis and other family members are buried.

---

[4]the way an area is decorated

28   There's more to see across the street at Graceland Plaza. This shopping mall contains several museums. They display 20 of Elvis's cars, his motorcycles, clothing, costumes, jewelry, and so on. In the souvenir shops, visitors can buy "treasures," such as a photocopy of an Elvis shopping list or some dirt from the Graceland property. One journalist bought a thank you note that Elvis had written to his cleaners. At Heartbreak Hotel Restaurant, tourists can sample recipes from the Presley family cookbook.

29   Elvis's two airplanes are in the parking lot. Visitors can go inside the *Lisa Marie*, his "penthouse in the sky." Elvis bought it from Delta Airlines for $1 million. It has a bedroom, dining room, and conference room, plus a shower.

Elvis's airplane, the Lisa Marie, *named after his daughter*

Checking Comprehension

Why did the Music Gate need frequent repairs?

What does Graceland's interior reveal about Elvis's lifestyle and tastes?

What can tourists buy to remember their visit?

---

30 One journalist pointed out that dying turned out to be a "good career move" for Elvis. Why? Elvis has earned more money and respect since his death than he had at the end of his career.

31 Although he'd earned billions during his lifetime, Elvis died leaving an estate worth only about $5 million. Much of his money had been spent, given away, or lost in bad investments. The upkeep of Graceland was high. So, in 1982, under the guidance of Priscilla Presley, Elvis Presley Enterprises opened Graceland to the public. Since then, money has poured in from house tours, royalties[5] from products bearing his name, and souvenirs. Some say that by 1993, Presley's estate was worth $75 to $100 million.

32 Elvis's fans have been compared to the followers of a religious leader. They ignore his weaknesses and find inspiration in his strengths. Elvis's devotion to mother, God, and country were genuine and deep. He never liked to be called the King. To Elvis, there was only one king, the one in heaven. Elvis was generous and humble. He was always honest about his limitations. He admitted that he could play only three chords on the guitar. But he could do anything on the piano. Elvis gave the piano credit for his musical skill on the keyboard. He was always polite and didn't think that made him a sissy.

33 Once, the adult world considered Elvis a symbol of immorality.[6] But after his death, six countries issued postage stamps in his honor. In 1992, Americans were asked to vote on whether they preferred a picture of young Elvis or mature Elvis on a stamp. Young Elvis won by a landslide.

---

[5]payments made for use of an artist's work
[6]behavior considered wrong or improper

The U.S. Post Office printed 500 million stamps. They went on sale on Elvis's 58th birthday. Some fans put them on envelopes mailed to imaginary people at fake addresses. They wanted to get their letters back stamped "Return to Sender."[7]

Checking Comprehension

Why is Elvis's death considered by some to be "a good career move"?

Which image did Elvis's American fans prefer to see shown on a postage stamp? Why?

[7]the title of one of Elvis's best-selling records

SIDELIGHTS

About Memphis

Memphis is the largest city in Tennessee. It some-times compares itself to the Egyptian city from which it gets its name. The name means "place of good abode." Instead of the Nile River, Memphis, Tennessee, is on the Mississippi.

Major sites in Memphis include

- The Pyramid Arena, a steel-and-concrete, 33-story pyramid, seats 22,000 for music and sporting events.
- Beale Street, birthplace of the blues, is still a lively nightclub scene. Along with a bronze statue of W. C. Handy, Father of the Blues, Beale Street has a huge bronze statue of Elvis.
- The National Civil Rights Museum, located at the former Lorraine Hotel, is where Martin Luther King Jr. was assassinated in 1968.

About Tennessee, the Volunteer State

Tennessee stretches eastward from the Mississippi River to the Great Smoky Mountains. It's the site of the nation's most popular parks. The state's nick-name refers to its tradition of military honor and bravery. Its young men have volunteered in great numbers to defend their country. Tennessee has pro-duced many famous military men, including Andrew Jackson, Davy Crockett, and Sam Houston.

Making Inferences

Reread the paragraph(s) indicated after each statement.
Then decide if each statement is probably true or false.

_____ 1. In the 1950s, TV helped Elvis become nationally famous. (paragraphs 10–11)

_____ 2. Elvis was called the King of Rock 'n' Roll because he was the first person to use this style. (paragraph 12)

_____ 3. Elvis was a symbol of defiance, but he didn't defy the authority figures in his own life. (paragraphs 14, 16, 32)

_____ 4. Elvis didn't approve of the use of illegal drugs. (paragraphs 15, 18)

_____ 5. When he sang, Elvis shook his body a lot in order to shock and offend adults. (paragraph 17)

_____ 6. Elvis was generous with his money, but he didn't spend much on himself. (paragraphs 19, 20, 23, 29)

_____ 7. Graceland is decorated in a dignified, simple, elegant manner. (paragraphs 24–26)

_____ 8. Once, people thought Elvis was immoral. Today, some people think he's immortal. (paragraphs 22, 32–33)

Practicing Vocabulary

Circle the correct word to complete each sentence.

1. When Elvis died, his (estate, home, airplane, devotion) was worth about $5 million.
2. In the early 1950s, many adults thought that Elvis's wild movements would encourage (dramatic, immortal, typical, immoral) behavior.
3. Most people who go to Graceland are Elvis Presley's (fans, trophies, victims, friends).

4. An impersonator tries to (recognize, encourage, imitate, entertain) someone else.
5. A souvenir helps a person (forget, remember, repeat, regret).
6. Something that is priceless is (worthless, too valuable to set a price on, rather expensive, overpriced).

Talking It Over

1. The paint on Elvis's "solid gold" Cadillac contained diamond dust and gold flakes. Inside was a gold-plated TV set, telephone, and razor. Why do you think Elvis wanted a car like this?
2. How would your life change if you earned as much as Elvis did?
3. Does great wealth bring problems?
4. Elvis once gave his manager a book. The cover said, "All I Learned from Colonel Tom Parker in Twenty Years by Elvis Presley." All the pages were blank! What does this reveal about Elvis?

Hot-air balloons in New Mexico

ENCHANTED LAND

What's the most photographed sporting event in the world? To find out, read on. . . .

Wild Places, Open Spaces

1 "If you ever go to New Mexico, it will itch you for the rest of your life." So said Georgia O'Keeffe, one of America's greatest modern artists. She first visited the state in 1929. Later, she left her husband for long periods to live in this quiet desert area. Bright, clear light, wide open spaces, and beautiful scenery inspired O'Keeffe's greatest work.

2 New Mexico has been attracting artists for the past century. More recently, its clear air and large, unpopulated areas have also brought scientists. In 1930, Robert Goddard, the rocket scientist, came to New Mexico to launch his missiles. (His Massachusetts neighbors had found his launchings too close for comfort.) In addition, research on the atomic bomb was conducted at Los Alamos. In 1945, the world's first atomic explosion took place at Trinity Site, about 60 miles from Alamogordo. Today, New Mexico remains a leading center of nuclear and space research.

3 In area, New Mexico is the nation's fifth largest state. But the population density averages only 13 people per square mile. Nearly half of New Mexicans live in or near

Albuquerque [Al'buh·ker·key], Las Cruces [Kru'says], or Santa Fe. Though the state has high mountains, in many places the empty desert seems endless.

4   New Mexico charms the art admirer, the science buff,[1] the history lover, and the performing arts fan. The scenery is breathtaking. The climate is warm and dry. And the mix of cultures creates great variety in museums, shops, food, architecture, and festivals. Where else can tourists attend Native American dances, Mexican fiestas, rodeos, and outdoor opera all on the same vacation?

Checking Comprehension

What draws artists to New Mexico?
Who were Robert Goddard and Georgia O'Keeffe?
Why is New Mexico thinly populated?

A Salad Bowl

5   New Mexico has been a state since 1912 and an American territory since 1848. Three major cultures—Hispanic, Native American, and Anglo (English-speaking Americans)—come together. This state has the highest percentages of Hispanics (37 percent) and Native Americans (9 percent) of any state. But New Mexico isn't a melting pot. It's more like a salad bowl. Cultures meet but never lose their identities.

6   In some northern counties, the Hispanic population exceeds 80 percent. The state's Mexican-American population is about 200,000. Spanish is spoken throughout the state. And the Hispanic influence is obvious in street names, churches, and foods.

---

[1] a person interested in and knowledgeable about a subject

7   The Native Americans of New Mexico live mainly on 5 reservations and 19 pueblos [pwe′blowz].[2] The Navajo [Na′vuh·ho] reservation, home of the largest Indian group in the United States, covers 16 million acres in New Mexico, Arizona, and Utah. Mescalero Apaches own ½ million acres in southeastern New Mexico. On it, they run a famous resort, the Inn of the Mountain Gods. Tourists often visit Indian reservations and pueblos. They watch Native American ceremonies and buy handmade Indian products. These include silver and turquoise [tur′koyz][3] jewelry, baskets, pottery, and blankets.

8   The name Pueblo was actually given to some New Mexican Indians by the Spanish. Their villages were called pueblos. So the Spanish called the people Pueblos. Missionaries[4]

Contemporary and historic collectibles at Tanner Chaney Gallery in Old Town, Albuquerque

---

[2]Native American villages with buildings made of stone or adobe (sun-dried clay bricks and mud)
[3]a greenish blue or sky blue semiprecious stone
[4]people sent to convert others to their religion

had trouble pronouncing Indian names. So they gave the villages Spanish names, after Christian saints. Each pueblo sets aside a special day to honor its patron saint. Native Americans honor Christian saints with ceremonial dances to buffalo, deer, corn, or the harvest. Tourists enjoy watching these festivities.

9   New Mexican food also reflects the blend of cultures. Mexican dishes such as tacos and enchiladas are served everywhere. *Sopaipilla* [so·pah·pee'yuh][5] is a popular treat. Recalling the diet of the pioneers, some New Mexican restaurants serve buffalo stew, steaks, and hamburgers. Corn, a staple of the Indian diet, is also basic to New Mexican cooking today. Navajo fry bread is served at pueblos, especially during festivals.

10   The New Mexican dining experience adds homegrown products. The state tree, the piñon, supplies piñon nuts. They're eaten raw and cooked in sauces and sweets. Some types of cactus bear fruit that makes good jelly. As in Mexico, chilis are used to season all kinds of dishes. More tons and varieties of chilis are grown in New Mexico than anywhere else in the world.

Checking Comprehension

Why is New Mexico compared to a salad bowl?
What facts show the state's multicultural character?
What are the major ethnic groups?
Name four influences on the New Mexican diet.

_____

[5]a puffy fried bread covered with honey

A Long History

11   New Mexico was home to some of the earliest North American residents. They lived there as early as 20,000 B.C. Native Americans called Anasazi [An·uh·sah'zee] lived in New Mexico by A.D. 1000. This advanced culture built multistory buildings that housed thousands. They had stations for observing the solar system, a complex network of roads, and many trade contacts. The Chaco Culture National Historic Park contains the remains of Pueblo Bonito. It was an apartment house with about 800 rooms!

12   By A.D. 1500, Apaches and Navajos roamed the area. Pueblo Indians (descendants of the Anasazi) grew corn, beans, and squash along the Rio Grande [Ree'oh Grahn'day].

13   The first European settlements were set up by the Spanish in 1598 and 1610. The region remained under Spanish rule for about 200 years. Then, in the early 1820s, it became part of a newly independent Mexico. After the Mexican War, the area became part of the United States.

14   New Mexico's history includes many bloody battles between Native American, Hispanic, and American forces. From these battles came some very famous names in 19th-century American history. They include the Apache warrior Geronimo and the famous explorer, soldier, and Indian fighter Kit Carson.

Checking Comprehension

How many different countries have controlled New Mexico since the 17th century?

What skills did the Anasazi have?

Were the Pueblo Indians wandering tribes?

---

15   Albuquerque is New Mexico's largest city by far. Its population is about 385,000. Every year, 4.5 million tourists visit. On the tourist trail, the first stop is often Old Town. This section has about 150 shops and art galleries in historic adobe [uh·doe'bee] buildings. On narrow, winding streets, shops sell Native American crafts. Wooden dolls that represent Pueblo Indian gods are popular collectors' items. So are the storyteller figures. These show an adult telling children the tribal legends.

16   On the Sandia Peak Aerial Tramway, tourists climb a 10,000-foot mountain in 20 minutes. This 2.7-mile journey up the jagged Sandia Mountains is the longest tram ride in the world. The ride takes climbers through four of the

Sandia Peak Aerial Tramway

earth's five zones.[6] It's like going from Mexico to Alaska in 20 minutes. Riders may see bears, sheep, and deer on the way up. From the top, they look down on half of New Mexico.

17   What else does Albuquerque offer tourists? Petroglyph National Monument has thousands of ancient drawings chipped into hardened lava. The Indian Pueblo and Cultural Center exhibits the best arts and crafts from all 19 pueblos. The New Mexico Museum of Natural History has a "live" volcano and exhibits about the age of dinosaurs.

18   The Albuquerque International Balloon Fiesta is one of the city's best fairs. It features more than 650 colorful hot-air balloons. About 1.5 million spectators come to watch. Some say this nine-day October fiesta is the world's most photographed sporting event. It gives Albuquerque its nickname, the Hot-Air Balloon Capital of the World.

19   Throughout the year when the weather is cool enough, licensed balloonists take tourists aloft. The best times to go up are just before daybreak and after sunset. That's when visibility is best and the air is the coolest. It's very quiet in the sky, except for blasts of flame that heat the air in the balloon. The usual trip takes passengers up 500 to 1,000 feet. That's high enough to see the balloon's shadow on the clouds below. But with special equipment, a hot-air balloon can go as high as 13,000 feet.

Checking Comprehension

What are two unusual things about the Sandia Peak Aerial Tramway ride?

Why is Albuquerque known as the Hot-Air Balloon Capital of the World?

[6]any of the five great divisions of the earth's surface with respect to latitude and temperature

20   Santa Fe, "the city different," is 7,000 feet above sea level at the base of 13,000-foot mountains. Two rivers are nearby. The Rio Grande is used for white-water rafting most of the year. The region's volcanic past left natural hot springs. Prehistoric Indians looked for health cures there, as people do today.

21   For a city of only 56,500 residents, Santa Fe has a number of cultural attractions. Its open-air summer opera and its symphony orchestra are outstanding. It has the world's largest museum of folk art and four major museums of American Indian art. Its fine arts museum has 8,000 works by regional artists.

22   Santa Fe is the nation's second oldest city (after St. Augustine, Florida) and the oldest capital city. In 1610, it was the capital of a Spanish province.[7] The city's Palace of Governors was built in 1610. It is the oldest government building in the United States. Now, it's a history museum, too. Native Americans sit on blankets under its columned porch and sell jewelry. By 1593, the nation's oldest road built by Europeans reached Santa Fe. El Camino Real [El Kah·mee'no Ray·el'] stretched from Santa Fe to Mexico City, Mexico. A part of this old route is now a street near the center of Santa Fe.

23   Santa Fe has a miraculous stairway and a story to go with it. In 1873, Loretto Chapel was being built for the area's first nuns. Suddenly, the architect died. The stairway to the choir loft didn't fit. The nuns prayed for a solution to this problem. One day, a carpenter arrived. In six months, he built a spiral stairway with two 360-degree turns and no central support. Then he left without waiting for payment.

24   Santa Fe's architecture blends Pueblo and Spanish styles with modern designs. This type of architecture is

[7]a part of a country

called Pueblo, Territorial, or Santa Fe. The city's oldest buildings are adobe. In 1957, Santa Fe passed a strict building code for its historic districts. Its purpose was to save the city's traditional style. However, today, many Santa Fe buildings that look adobe are really wood frame.

Checking Comprehension

What do tourists do in Santa Fe?
What's strange about Loretto Chapel's stairway?

Taos

25 Taos [Tah'os], 70 miles north of Santa Fe, is a community of about 4,000 people. But this little town is world famous as an artists' colony, a ski resort, and an important Indian site. Taos Pueblo is one of the oldest continuously inhabited communities in the United States. The buildings, at least 700 years old, are the best example of multistory pueblo buildings still standing. Today, only 200 Indians live in

Taos Pueblo

these old buildings. They have no electricity, phones, or indoor plumbing. About 2,000 other tribal members live in modern homes elsewhere on the 102,000-acre reservation.

26   Kit Carson's Taos home is now a museum open to the public. Carson was a trapper, guide, and government agent. His work involved fighting Indians and forcing them onto reservations. But he liked and respected Native Americans and hated this job. When he returned home to Taos, he handled Indian affairs for the Colorado Territory and tried to help Indians.

27   No doubt, Kit Carson would delight in New Mexico today. The bloody battles between ethnic groups are history. Today, this multicultural state takes pride in its diversity.[8] New Mexico is eager to share its various cultures with tourists. The state motto is "We grow as we go." A visit to New Mexico certainly is a growing experience. The state's nickname is also perfect. New Mexico is, indeed, a Land of Enchantment.

Checking Comprehension

Why is Taos a famous community?
How did Kit Carson feel about American Indians?
What are some things visitors to New Mexico learn about?

---

[8]variety, differences

SIDELIGHTS

About Other New Mexican Sites

- **Carlsbad Caverns National Park:** This chain of huge underground rooms has oddly shaped, colorful limestone formations. Some caves are the summer homes of 300,000 bats! They fly out at dusk to hunt for food and turn the sky black.
- **White Sands National Monument:** The largest gypsum dune field in the world, it occupies 330 square miles. The soft, white, glistening sand looks like ocean waves.
- **International Space Hall of Fame:** Exhibits, games, films, laser light shows, and a planetarium all tell about space exploration.
- **Smokey Bear Historical State Park:** In 1950, after an accidental forest fire, Smoky was found here, a burned cub clinging to a tree. He became the major symbol for fire safety. A nature trail leads to his gravesite.

About New Mexico, Land of Enchantment

Although fifth in size among the 50 states, New Mexico ranks 37th in population with only 1.5 million residents. The state is rich in natural resources, such as oil and natural gas. Its major crops include peanuts, pecans, apples, cotton, and chilis. The state bird is the roadrunner. Roadrunners often chase people and cars—running a brisk 15 miles an hour!

Making Inferences

Reread the paragraph(s) indicated after each statement.
Then decide if each statement is probably true or false.

_____ 1. The Georgia O'Keeffe quotation that begins the reading suggests that the state's dry air made her skin itch. (paragraph 1)

_____ 2. Scientists came to New Mexico for some of the same reasons that artists did. (paragraph 2)

_____ 3. New Mexico has more Hispanic residents than any other state. (paragraph 5)

_____ 4. New Mexican food is the same as Mexican food. (paragraphs 9–10)

_____ 5. The Anasazi lived in New Mexico about 3,000 years ago. (paragraph 11)

_____ 6. Hot-air balloons can go above the clouds. (paragraph 19)

_____ 7. Kit Carson lived in Taos Pueblo. (paragraph 26)

Practicing Vocabulary

Circle the correct word(s) to complete each sentence.

1. Pueblo Indians built their homes of (clay and mud, animal skins, steel, ice).
2. Many New Mexican Indians live in (resorts, pueblos, unpopulated areas, research centers).
3. New Mexican cooks often season their food with (chilis, pottery, turquoise, corn).
4. The top of the Sandia Mountains is its (province, peak, loft, site).
5. New Mexico is proud of its ethnic (scenery, diversity, balloonists, caverns).

Talking It Over

1. At one time, all Native Americans lived on reservations. Is this true today?
2. Why is Santa Fe called "the city different"? In what ways is it unusual?
3. Would you like to go up in a hot-air balloon? Why or why not? Would you be able to control the balloon's height and direction? How do you think that is done?
4. New Mexico's population has been growing rapidly since 1970. Why do you think people are attracted to this state?
5. Was the invention of the atomic bomb progress? What other scientific advancements have proved to be dangerous or harmful to society? Is scientific change good or evil?

Waikiki Beach, Hawaii

ALOHA!

Which islands are actually the crests of an underwater mountain range? To find out, read on. . . .

Maui and Pele

1   A Polynesian god, Maui [Maw'ee], and his brothers are said to have pulled the Hawaiian Islands up off the ocean floor with a fish hook. Maui warned his brothers not to be curious. They weren't supposed to look back at what they were discovering. When they did, they were punished. Instead of creating a solid land mass, they made a series of islands. Today, Hawaii is a chain of 132 islands. But the four million visitors a year usually see the 5 main islands: Hawaii, Maui, Molokai [Mah·luh·kigh'], Oahu [O·ah'hu], and Kauai [Kow'eye].

2   Hawaii lies in the Pacific Ocean, 2,000 miles southwest of California. It's spread over 1,523 miles of water. But, in land area, Hawaii is very small. It ranks 47th in size among the states. Many of its islands—124 in all—are atolls, small coral reefs. Only birds and small sea creatures can live on an atoll.

3   The Hawaiian Islands are actually the tip of the biggest mountain range on earth. This range lies on the ocean floor. It was created by volcanoes millions of years ago. Even today, it continues to grow and change.

4   In geologic time, America's 50th state is a mere baby.

The continents were formed more than 300 million years ago. But most of the islands of Hawaii pushed up out of the sea only 25 million years ago. The oldest part of Maui is only 2 million years old. Other parts of the island are only 200 years old.

5   The process of change continues on the islands because of two active volcanoes, Mauna Loa [Maw'nuh Low'uh] and Kilauea [Key·luh·way'uh]. Both of these volcanoes are on the main island of Hawaii, called the Big Island. Mauna Loa, with an elevation of 13,680 feet, is three times higher than Kilauea. Many visitors are surprised when they see Kilauea. It looks like a small dent in Mauna Loa's side rather than a separate volcanic mountain.

Kilauea volcano erupts in Hawaii.

6   One of the most popular places for tourists is the Hawaii Volcanoes National Park. Established in 1916, the park allows visitors to see the colorful but rather quiet volcanoes perform. Some people stay for a few hours. Others camp on the site itself. As tourists hike through the park, they see places where basins, called craters, have formed. These craters were made when volcanoes erupted. Tourists also see steam puffing out of cracks in the hardened lava.[1] New lava flows gently down the slopes in wide red rivers. But at night, the lava can also look blue, purple, orange, and green. Tourists explore the craters and watch the steam. Piles of rocks guide visitors to the mouth of the volcano!

7   According to Polynesian myth, Pele, goddess of fire, lives at the mouth of a huge crater. Long ago, Pele was trying to escape from her cruel sister, the goddess of the ocean. First she tried other craters, but her sister ruined them with storms. Finally, safe on the Big Island, Pele rested. Pele still fears her sister's power, so she sends lava down the cliffs into the ocean. Several times, long ago, people were caught in fatal lava flows. Usually Pele is more peaceful. Island natives describe her as an ancient, wrinkled woman who must be respected.

Checking Comprehension

According to myth, who is Maui? How did he and his brothers create the islands?

What causes constant changes on the Hawaiian Islands?

Why, by geologic time, is Hawaii a baby?

---

[1]melted rock which has spilled on the ground

8   No one lived on the Hawaiian Islands until 1,200 years ago. Then, people from the South Pacific, called Polynesians, built huge canoes. They sailed from the South Pacific more than 2,000 miles to Hawaii. They used the stars, the currents, and bird migrations to guide them. They brought pigs, dogs, and coconuts with them on their voyage. They built houses and temples made of stone on the islands of Hawaii.

9   A second group of sailors came from Tahiti [Teh·he'tee] about 500 years later. These people worshipped different gods with magic powers. These gods were called *mana*. At the temples they built, *kahuna*, or priests, sacrificed plants, animals, and sometimes people to assure good weather and good fishing. Today, at Hawaii Volcanoes National Park, tourists can visit a temple and learn how the early inhabitants wove baskets, fished, and told stories in song and dance.

10   Many Polynesians and Tahitians intermarried. They lived on the islands for 500 years before an Englishman, Captain James Cook, came to Hawaii in January of 1778. He landed on Kauai. At first, the natives worshipped him. They thought he was the ancient god of peace and fertility. He named the islands the Sandwich Islands after the Earl of Sandwich, who had sponsored his voyage. Our word *sandwich* comes from this famous earl. He liked to gamble so much that sandwiches were invented so he could keep gambling even while he was eating!

11   When Cook arrived, 250,000 natives were living on the Hawaiian Islands. Their powerful king united the islands under one government for the first time. Part of the king's success at this involved the volcano, Kilauea. It erupted while he was fighting a local chief. The chief's soldiers were

killed by the eruption. So the people on the island of Hawaii thought that the goddess Pele favored the king.

12   Cook opened the island to visits by France, Russia, Spain, Portugal, and the United States. Hawaii was an ideal place to stop on the way to Asia. Many ships restocked in Hawaii. They also traded the spices, silks, and tea of the East for the furs of the American northwest and Europe. But European trade also brought new illnesses. More than three-quarters of the native inhabitants caught diseases formerly unknown on the islands. By 1872, only one-quarter of the Hawaiian Islanders were still alive.

13   Through the first half of the 19th century, Hawaiian royalty, British soldiers, and American missionaries fought for power. Meanwhile, the sugar planters, who owned large plantations, tried to change the laws of ownership. At that time, the royal family owned all the land. A law was passed in 1850. It let citizens own the small pieces of land they were living on. It also allowed foreigners to own land for the first time. One wealthy American landowner, Sanford B. Dole, overthrew the weak native queen. Then he declared himself president of Hawaii. In 1896, Hawaii became a possession of the United States and, in 1900, a territory. Dole became its first governor. (We still see his family's name today on the many pineapple products grown in Hawaii.) It would take nearly 60 more years for Hawaii to become a state.

Checking Comprehension

How do we know that the early Polynesian settlers were good navigators?

Why was a volcanic eruption important to the history of the islands?

Why was Hawaii an ideal place for trading ships to stop?

14   Since World War II, Hawaii has become one of the most popular tourist sites in the world. About 100,000 people a day visit Hawaii. Tourists add $3 billion a year to the local economy. How did this remote group of islands become such a popular tourist site? Soldiers who served in the Pacific became familiar with its beauty and charm. The U.S. military provided the islands with several airports. These airports opened Hawaii to commercial travel. After the war, film, radio, and television personalities publicized Hawaiian culture. Wearing colorful, flower-patterned Hawaiian shirts and leis [layz],[2] they strummed ukuleles [yuke·uh·lay′leez][3] and sang about the island. Actually, the instrument was imported from Portugal. Only its name is Hawaiian.

15   At the beginning of the tourist boom, Honolulu, on the island of Oahu, had only five hotels. Since then, hundreds have been built. Another popular tourist attraction also opened. The Ala Moana Shopping Center was the largest shopping center in the world when it opened in 1959.

16   But most visitors don't come to Hawaii to shop. They come to enjoy the tropical sun, the fragrant, flower-scented air, and the wonderful beaches. Surfing, or wave sliding, is Hawaii's oldest sport. It was imported by the Polynesians. They practiced it in ancient times. Surfing today is an internationally competitive activity. Waikiki ("spouting

---

[2] floral necklaces
[3] small four-stringed instruments shaped like a guitar

water") Beach is one of the most popular surfing beaches in the world. As far back as the 1500s, chants and songs were sung about Waikiki surfers. Even Captain Cook remarked about their bold and dangerous stunts. Other water sports popular in Hawaii are sailing, canoeing, snorkeling, and scuba and deep-sea diving.

17　　　Athletic tourists also find a variety of other sports to keep them entertained. Biking, hiking, tennis, and golf are equally popular. Horseback riding allows people to see the more remote parts of the islands. Sports such as basketball, baseball, and football are also practiced. In fact, the Pro Bowl game takes place in Aloha Stadium, Honolulu. A tourist might guess that every sport but snow skiing is practiced in Hawaii. But on the island of Hawaii, from January to March, there is enough snow to ski on Mauna Kea.

Checking Comprehension

Why did tourism increase after World War II?
What sports are most popular in Hawaii?

---

18 A visit to Hawaii wouldn't be complete without dancing the hula. Believe it or not, in the 1800s, missionaries outlawed the hula as an obscene[4] and politically dangerous dance. It wasn't revived until 1915.

19 The dance features hand gestures that tell a story and offer prayers for future success. At every major hotel on the islands, hula dancing is practiced. Tourists, wearing colorful flowered cotton or grass skirts, learn the dance. But there are also university courses in the tradition of the dance. Hula scholars study it seriously.

Hula dancers tell a story with hand gestures.

20 A typical hula dancer wears leis made of flowers and leaves as well as seeds and berries. The fancier the leis, the more honored the guest. Popular lei-making classes are

---

[4]vulgar, dirty

offered. Each of the islands has its own style of necklace. Some islands use shells. Others use fruits, vines, roses, orchids, and even moss.

21   Hawaiians often have luaus [loo'owz], or feasts, on important occasions such as marriages. Tourists can enjoy a special luau any night in many Hawaiian hotels. Along with the colorful fire dancers and drummers, some tourist luaus feature actors dressed as sailors, native kings and queens, Captain Cook, and missionaries. Many tourist luaus are sing-alongs. The audience is taught modern favorites such as "Blue Hawaii," as well as more traditional songs. Buses, horses, and hay wagons take guests to the many hotel luaus.

22   *Onolicious* is the term that Hawaiians use to describe the food served at these big dinners. "Ono," which means "good" in Hawaiian, is combined with the English word *delicious*. *Onolicious* includes *kalua* pig, which is roasted underground on hot stones for at least five hours. Other local favorites are *poi*, made from a root called *taro*. Many visitors think *poi* tastes like paste. They eat it in small amounts on pig or salmon. The luau also features salmon in tomato and onion sauce, chicken with pineapple and coconut milk. Just as Hawaii blends cultures, it also blends food. Japanese, Portuguese, Korean, and Chinese favorites also decorate the big buffet tables.

Checking Comprehension

What are hulas, leis, *poi*, and luaus?
Why was the hula banned in Hawaii?
What are some of the foods served in Hawaii?

Sacrifices and Courage

23 Not all of the tourist sites and activities in Hawaii are associated with pleasure. One of the most popular places to visit on Molokai is Father Damien's leper[5] colony. Here, lepers were isolated on a high, lonely cliff. Father Damien, a Belgian priest, came in the late 19th century to help the lepers. Visits to the colony include a tour of Father Damien's church and the ruins of more than 300 Hawaiian structures.

24 The evolution[6] of Hawaiian religious history can be seen on Molokai's southern coast. In the 1300s, Hawaii's largest temple was built of huge stones brought there one by one. It was used for human sacrifice. Also present on the coast are several of Father Damien's white wooden churches. There, missionaries introduced Christianity to the people.

25 Another national park on the island of Hawaii is a former religious site. It is a city with black lava walls. Warriors and islanders who had broken taboos or laws went there to escape. In the 16th century, taboos included eating with members of the opposite sex and walking too close to the chief. Breaking these laws could result in the death penalty! Getting to the refuge[7] took great courage. People trying to escape had to use a boat or swim in dangerous waters to this remote outpost. Today, the park is a living museum of native life. Costumed islanders weave baskets, carve wood, make sandals and leis, and fish the old-fashioned way—with nets.

---

[5] a person with a disease that causes large sores, paralysis, and muscle loss
[6] change through time
[7] a place of safety

26   At the end of Waikiki Beach on Oahu is Diamond Head, a volcanic crater. Diamond Head got its name from British sailors. They thought the crystal deposits at its crater were diamonds. This crater was the site of the last human sacrifices on the island. After a battle in 1795, the ruler commanded that warriors be sacrificed there. The Hawaiian name for the popular site is Laeahi [Lay·ah'hee], or "brow of the tuna." Legend says it was named by Pele's younger sister. She thought the crater's profile looked like a golden tuna.

27   Another tragic human sacrifice took place at Pearl Harbor, also on Oahu. The U.S.S. *Arizona* memorial is a reminder of December 7, 1941, the day that 343 Japanese bombers attacked Pearl Harbor. The bombing sank the ship and killed 1,177 of its crew. This attack also damaged three more ships and killed 2,403 men. It caused the United States to enter World War II. The hull[8] of the ship lies in 38 feet of water, but above water is the U.S.S. *Arizona* memorial. Inside is a white marble shrine that lists the names of the men who lost their lives.

U.S.S. Arizona *Memorial*

---

[8]the frame or body of a ship

28   In addition to the monument, an exhibit explains America's involvement in the war in the Pacific. The museum contains items salvaged[9] from the ship. It also has photographs, uniforms, and model ships. A film explains the history of the ship and tells the story of the attack. More than 4,000 tourists a day visit this memorial.

29   From the volcanoes to the beautiful waters to the U.S.S. *Arizona* monument, Hawaii offers tourists a chance to see time pass in many ways—geologic time, recreational time, and historical time. Most people who visit Hawaii come back again. They say the Aloha State grows more fascinating with each visit.

Checking Comprehension

Who was Father Damien?

What is a taboo?

What happened after the Japanese bombed Pearl Harbor?

---

[9]rescued or saved from a wreck

SIDELIGHTS

About Hawaii, the Aloha State

- About the state's nickname: *Aloha* means "hello," "love," and "goodbye." In Hawaiian, *alo-* means "to face" and *ha* means "the breath of life."
- Hawaii became the 50th state in 1959.
- One million people live on the islands. Forty percent are Asian: 23 percent are Japanese, 11 percent are Philippino, and 4.5 percent are Chinese. One-third of Hawaiians are Caucasian. Samoans, African-Americans, and Puerto Ricans make up the rest of the population.
- Its main products are sugar cane, coffee, pineapple, macadamia nuts, and melons.
- Hawaiian and English are the official languages of Hawaii.
- Nine daily newspapers are published in Hawaii: six in English, one in Japanese and English, one in Korean, and one in Chinese.

About the Islands

Each major island has a nickname:

- Kauai is the Garden Island.
- Oahu is the Gathering Place.
- Molokai is the Friendly Isle.
- Maui is the Mountain Island or Magic Island.
- Hawaii is the Big Island.

Making Inferences

Reread the paragraph(s) indicated after each statement.
Then decide if each statement is probably true or false.

_____ 1. The stories of Maui and Pele are true because
they are myths. (paragraphs 1, 7)

_____ 2. Two thousand years ago, the Hawaiian Islands
were uninhabited. (paragraph 8)

_____ 3. Without airports, tourism wouldn't have
increased in Hawaii. (paragraph 14)

_____ 4. Snow skiing is one of the most popular sports in
Hawaii. (paragraph 17)

_____ 5. Missionaries enjoyed the stories and prayers told
by the hula. (paragraph 18)

_____ 6. Like the story of Hawaii itself, the story of the
U.S.S. *Arizona* is both above and below water.
(paragraphs 3, 27–28)

Practicing Vocabulary

Circle the correct word to complete each sentence.

1. Maui and his brothers created the Hawaiian Islands.
Because his brothers were (curious, brave, competitive,
bold), the land surfaced as a series of islands.
2. Hawaii is actually one huge (volcano, crater, atoll,
mountain) range sitting on the ocean floor.
3. (Hulas, Leis, *Poi*, Luaus) tell stories and wishes for the
future.
4. Father Damien (toured, celebrated, traded, sacrificed)
his life for the sake of the lepers on Molokai.
5. Taboos should not be (sacrificed, broken, celebrated,
salvaged).
6. After the U.S.S. *Arizona* sank in Pearl Harbor, many
items were (sacrificed, celebrated, salvaged, visited)
from it.

Talking It Over

1. Why do people create myths and legends such as the ones about Maui and Pele?
2. Do you know any myths and legends? Tell one.
3. Father Damien sacrificed his life for the sake of the lepers. The men at Pearl Harbor sacrificed their lives. Plants, animals, and people were sacrificed to the gods in Hawaiian history. Is death always a part of sacrifice? Is choice always a part of sacrifice?
4. Have you ever sacrificed something? What was it? Did you do it willingly or unwillingly?
5. Are there still taboos in modern American culture? What are some?
6. What do you think attracts tourists to volcanic sites: scientific interest or danger? Would you visit one of the volcanoes?
7. What part of Hawaiian native culture interests you most? Why?

Paramount Studios in Hollywood, California

LA LA LAND

A famous star stepped in the wrong place and
started a Hollywood tradition. What was it?
To find out, read on. . . .

Hollywoodland

1   The name Hollywood has long been connected with the
American movie industry. But the name reached southern
California before the movie industry did. In 1887, Mr. and
Mrs. Harvey Wilcox came from Ohio to the Los Angeles
area. They founded their dream city on a 200-acre fig and
apricot ranch. Then, on a train ride back to the Midwest,
Mrs. Wilcox met a Chicago-area woman who owned a
country estate named *Hollywood*. Mrs. Wilcox fell in love
with the name and brought it back to her little community.
She also provided Hollywood with its first sidewalks, bank,
post office, churches, and theater.

2   Hollywood's famous sign was first built in 1923. Orig-
inally, it didn't have any connection to movies. In those
days, the sign said *Hollywoodland*. It was put up to adver-
tise a housing development. In 1949, *Hollywoodland* was
shortened to *Hollywood*. In 1973, the sign became a national landmark.

3   A few years later, the famous sign began to show its
age. The Los Angeles Chamber of Commerce raised money
to rebuild it. The cost was $27,500 per letter! Many dona-

tions came from famous stars. Today's sign, made of metal covered with white baked enamel,[1] is very durable.[2] Each letter is 50 feet high and 30 feet wide. The sign sits high on a hill one mile east of the famous street corner Hollywood and Vine. Even through L.A.'s thick smog,[3] it can be seen for miles.

4   When visitors come to Hollywood today, they see a run-down neighborhood. But that doesn't seem to matter. Hollywood the movie industry is what's important. To what extent does southern California still dominate the movie industry? About 400 full-length films are made in the United States each year. Roughly half of these are made by the eight major studios based in southern California. About 100 movies are filmed in southern California annually. Movies are made all over the country. But L.A. is still the country's filmmaking center, as well as its recording and TV center. Every year, more than 100 TV dramas and situation comedies are made in California, mostly in or near L.A. No wonder it's called the world's entertainment capital.

5   Lately, L.A. has been given a new nickname: La La Land. That name may suggest too much fun and a lack of serious interests. But in southern California fun *is* serious business.

Checking Comprehension

Which came first, the name Hollywood or the Los Angeles movie industry?

Who paid to rebuild the aging Hollywood sign?

What are the three major entertainment industries in Los Angeles?

---

[1]a smooth, hard, shiny, paintlike coating
[2]long-lasting, even when used often
[3]a mixture of smoke and fog

6   In the late 1800s, the movie camera and projector were developed. By 1908, about 10 million Americans were spending their nickels and dimes to see movies. Most of the early silent movies were made in New York or Chicago. The first movies about the American West were actually filmed in New Jersey! But southern California's mild climate and varied landscape made it a much better choice for film-making. Hollywood's first movie was made in 1911. Its first full-length film came out in 1913.

7   World War I almost destroyed Europe's young film industry. By 1919, Hollywood was the movie capital of the world. Four out of every five films were produced there. Talking movies were introduced in 1927. By the 1930s, many American film stars were known worldwide.

8   In the 1920s, two fancy movie theaters were built on Hollywood Boulevard—the Chinese Theater and the Egyptian Theater. Movie premieres[4] were held at both. The stars of the films attended the openings and were surrounded by big crowds of fans.

9   Soon after the Chinese Theater opened in 1927, a famous star named Norma Talmadge stepped into some wet cement in front of the building. Her accident started a tradition. More than 200 stars have left their marks in the cement in front of this theater. Most of the square blocks contain signatures above handprints and/or footprints. But some stars added more. Roy Rogers, a movie cowboy, left the imprint of his gun and the hoofprint of his horse, Trigger. Jimmy Durante left the outline of his huge nose. Anthony Quinn left a message—"Dreams do come true."

---

[4]first performances

The footprints and handprints of actor John Travolta

Checking Comprehension

What two conditions made southern California a good place for making movies?

How did World War I affect the movie industry?

What accident happened at the Chinese Theater?

10   The Chinese Theater is a popular starting point for tourists. Movie fans photograph the cement blocks. They step into the footprints, and try the handprints out for size. Another attraction is the the Walk of Fame. It extends for two miles on Hollywood Boulevard and a few blocks on Vine Street. It has more than 2,500 pink stars in black squares. Most of them display an entertainer's name and the symbol of his or her entertainment medium. (It may be movies, radio, TV, theater, or records.) But there are still hundreds of nameless stars, waiting for the celebrities[5] of tomorrow. It's considered a great honor to have a star on the Walk of Fame. It also costs the performer about $5,000!

11   While touring Hollywood, visitors usually notice the Capitol Records Tower. It was the world's first round office building. It looks like a pile of phonograph records, with the spire on top as its needle. At night, a light on the roof flashes H-O-L-L-Y-W-O-O-D in Morse code. Tourists also visit Universal Studios Hollywood. Its 420-acre site is the largest complex of movie studios in the world. In addition, Universal is a theme park. As such, it is the biggest tourist attraction in southern California after Disneyland. On Universal's exciting train ride, passengers are threatened by a shark and an earthquake. The theme park also has stunt shows, animal shows, and exhibits on filmmaking. Few visitors actually see a movie star at work.

12   Another Hollywood tourist spot is full of stars—the Wax Museum. It is filled with life-sized figures made of wax. They look real—but they can't sign autographs. However, at the Hollywood Bowl, live stars appear regularly.

---

[5]famous people

They perform under the twinkling stars. Since 1922, open-air concerts, both popular and classical, have been held there. The Hollywood Bowl seats 17,000 in front of its bandshell.

13   The Hollywood Roosevelt Hotel is another landmark. In 1929, the first Oscars were presented there—in a ceremony open to the public. In 1985, the hotel underwent a $2 million restoration. Today, it is elegant once again. At one time, the greatest stars stayed there. On the mezzanine,[6] these great stars are featured in a large display of old photos.

14   As one might expect, there are several places to see movies in Hollywood. Silent comedies, new releases, even the latest 75-millimeter (wide-screen) films are shown. After a movie, tourists can still stop at C. C. Brown's Ice Cream Parlor. There, the hot fudge sundae was invented. And Judy Garland used to serve this special treat.

Checking Comprehension

What are the two famous attractions on the sidewalks of Hollywood?

What are some unusual features of the Capitol Records building?

Why do tourists go to Universal Studios Hollywood?

The Search Continues

15   Americans have always had great curiosity about the personal lives of movie stars. When they go to L.A., many people drive by the stars' homes. They can do this on a van tour or by car, following a "star map" with addresses of

---

[6]a story immediately above the first floor

famous entertainers. Many movie stars live in Beverly Hills, a separate town located inside L.A. Most stars have tall fences or high bushes around their homes for privacy.

16 Tour guides and guidebooks also mention the favorite restaurants, night clubs, and shopping areas of the stars. Many tourists go to these places in hopes of getting a star's photograph or autograph. Some fans go to a store called A Star is Worn to buy clothing once used in a movie. Others visit cemeteries where former stars are buried. Of all the deceased stars, Marilyn Monroe's gravesite is visited the most.

17 The search for celebrities continues on Beverly Hills's Rodeo [Roh·day'o] Drive. It's one of the most famous and most expensive shopping districts in the world. The shops there sell clothing, shoes, art, dishes, and jewelry. Very few stores put prices in the windows. But inside they have ties for $100, shoes for $400, and paintings for $20,000. To shop at one clothing store, customers must make an appointment.

18 Movie stars by the dozens are visible on the annual Academy Awards show, televised from L.A. Since 1929, the Academy of Motion Picture Arts and Sciences has given awards for outstanding work in all areas of filmmaking. Each winner receives a 13.5-inch, gold-plated statue called an *Oscar*. The names of the winners are kept secret until the awards are presented.

Checking Comprehension

Why don't the stores on Rodeo Drive put prices in their windows?

Why do some celebrities build fences around their property?

City of Angels

19   The city of Los Angeles has a population of 3.4 million. It lies within a county of 8.6 million and a five-county area of 14.5 million. In addition, 25 million visitors crowd into the area each year. They find much to enjoy. There are fine museums, art galleries, theme parks, beautiful scenery, and a wide variety of restaurants. L.A., the nation's second largest city in population, has a lot to offer both residents and tourists.

20   Surrounded by mountains on three sides, L.A. is very scenic. Its hills, valleys, canyons, and mountains are very beautiful. Colorful flowers brighten the landscape. Its tall palm trees, looking like rows of pencils, seem to brush the sky. L.A. weather is warm, sunny, and dry most of the time. The climate is great, residents claim. But is it? The summer heat brings smog. Heavy winter rains bring floods and mud slides. Earthquakes are common. An earthquake in January of 1994 destroyed thousands of homes and buildings and damaged parts of a major freeway.

21   L.A.'s ethnic diversity creates tensions as well as interesting dining spots. About 49 percent of the area's residents are white non-Hispanic and 33 percent are Hispanic. L.A.'s many ethnic neighborhoods include Olvera Street (Mexican), Chinatown, Little Tokyo, Koreatown, and Watts (mostly African-American).

22   Like other large American cities, L.A. has its share of problems. The public schools are overcrowded and underfunded. Crime and unemployment are high. Homes are very expensive. Also, there's not enough public transportation. The city covers 467 square miles; the county, about 4,000 square miles. To get from one place to another, a car is a necessity. But highway construction has not kept up

L.A. freeways overlapping

with population growth. So the city is famous for its traffic jams. Many drivers eat a meal, read the newspaper, talk on the telephone, or do crossword puzzles when they get stuck on the freeways.[7]

---

[7]free, limited-access, multiple-lane, divided highways

23   On weekends, L.A. residents (Angelenos) like to enjoy the outdoors. Southern California offers a lot to see and do outdoors, especially along the ocean. In Venice, for example, visitors walk along the ocean for blocks, shopping at outdoor stands. Roller skaters whiz by. Some people exercise while surfers ride the ocean waves. Musicians and jugglers perform in the streets in hopes of a handout.[8]

24   From Venice, vacationers can follow the Pacific Coast Highway in either direction: south toward San Diego or north toward San Francisco. Either way, the scenery is beautiful. Vacationers often spend several days driving along the ocean. They enjoy the beach, the mountains, and the interesting coastal towns. They may stop to view outdoor art exhibits, a common sight on weekends. Southern California's casual outdoor lifestyle and great beauty are very appealing. Many people who go there for a visit never go home again.

Checking Comprehension

Why is southern California a good vacation spot?
What are some disadvantages of the L.A. climate?
Why is L.A. a photographer's paradise?

---

[8]a donation of money

SIDELIGHTS

About Hollywood

- How big is Universal Studios Hollywood? The facility has 34 sound stages and a back lot with 573 buildings.
- How did the Oscar get its name? In 1931, the executive director of the Academy of Motion Picture Arts and Sciences took a close look at the statuette. It looked just like her Uncle Oscar!
- How many extras were the most ever used in a film? About 300,000 extras appeared in the funeral scene of *Gandhi.*
- How much do movies cost? The average cost of a movie produced by one of the eight major studios is $26 million.
- How much can a movie make? The most successful American films have grossed more than $700 million worldwide.

About California, the Golden State

California gets its nickname, the Golden State, from the state flower, golden poppies, and from the gold discovered there in 1848.

California has the largest population of the 50 states (about 30 million) and is third in area. Death Valley, 282 feet below sea level, is the lowest spot in the western hemisphere. Mount Whitney (14,491 feet high) is the highest point in the 48 connected states. Southern California's palm trees are also quite high. Most are 60 to 90 feet tall and some grow as tall as 120 feet.

Making Inferences

Reread the paragraph(s) indicated after each statement. Then decide if each statement is probably true or false.

_____ 1. Hollywood is a section of Los Angeles, not a separate city. (paragraphs 3–4)

_____ 2. The American film industry started in California. (paragraph 6)

_____ 3. Tourists sightseeing at Universal Studios Hollywood rarely see a movie star. (paragraph 11)

_____ 4. Movie stars keep their addresses secret. (paragraph 15)

_____ 5. Many people who don't act in movies receive Oscars. (paragraph 18)

_____ 6. Traffic on L.A. freeways always moves quickly. (paragraph 22)

Practicing Vocabulary

Part A. Circle the correct word to complete each sentence.

1. In front of the Chinese Theater, movie stars step into wet (enamel, cement, cemeteries, celebrities).
2. Movie stars don't have much privacy because they are (fans, elegant, residents, celebrities).
3. Americans who want to know about the personal lives of movie stars have a lot of (privacy, emphasis, curiosity, celebrities).
4. In the filmmaking industry, an Oscar is given for work that is (popular, outstanding, serious, elegant).
5. Sometimes the air in Los Angeles is unhealthy because of the (mountains, galleries, ceremonies, smog).

Part B. Tell the differences between the following pairs:

a country and a county
weather and climate
a visitor and a tourist
a signature and an autograph

Talking It Over

1. What's your favorite movie? What do you think makes a movie good?
2. What are the best traits of American movies? What are the worst? Do you like foreign films better? Why or why not?
3. Women who act now call themselves *actors* rather than *actresses*. Why do women dislike the word *actress*? What other words ending in *-ess* seem to be falling into disuse?
4. Why do you think fans want to see movie stars in person? Why do they ask for autographs?
5. Have you ever experienced severe weather conditions, such as an earthquake, tornado, hurricane, flood, blizzard, avalanche, or mud slide? If so, describe how you felt and what you did.

The Ice Castle at Winter Carnival in Minnesota

WINTER
WONDERLAND

Minnesota is often the coldest place in the United States.
What do you think was its coldest temperature ever?
To find out, read on. . . .

Icebox, U.S.A.

1   In Minnesota, winter is serious business. It is extremely cold and very snowy. How do residents cope? With imagination and a sense of humor.

2   International Falls, Minnesota, located in the northernmost portion of the state, borders Canada. Called "the icebox of the nation," this town often registers the lowest winter temperatures in the country. Its frigid climate inspired the name of Frostbite Falls, home of cartoon characters Rocky and Bullwinkle. It also has a giant thermometer, 22 feet high, which displays the current temperature. The town's coldest day was a bone-chilling −46° F!

3   Every January, the area sponsors Icebox Days. The 10-day festival includes the famous Freeze Yer Gizzard Blizzard Run. This 10-kilometer race is run no matter how cold it gets. There's also an unusual skiing race. Teams of four ski together on two long boards with eight tennis shoes.

4   St. Paul, Minnesota, residents and visitors brave the cold to enjoy Winter Carnival, an annual event since 1886.

In late January and early February, the nation's oldest and largest winter carnival attracts 1.5 million visitors a year. They come to see the fabulous ice and snow sculptures.

5   At the 1989 Winter Carnival, Chinese ice carvers sculpted a 50-foot ice dragon. In 1990, carnival sculptors built a snowman taller than a six-story building. In 1992, the Carnival's main attraction was the Ice Castle, built with 18,000 ice blocks. Standing 150 feet high, it was the tallest ice structure in the world.

Checking Comprehension

Why is International Falls well known?

What unusual winter events do Minnesotans enjoy?

Outdoor Sports Move Indoors

6   Minnesota residents got tired of cancelling sporting events because of severe winter weather. So, in 1982, Minneapolis became the site of the Hubert H. Humphrey Metrodome. It is the world's largest indoor, air-supported, multiple-use stadium. It's named after Senator Humphrey of Minnesota, vice president of the United States from 1964 to 1968.

7   In this gigantic stadium, athletes run on artificial grass. They also have a domed roof over their heads. About 250,000 cubic feet of air pressure holds up the fiberglass dome. When a game is over, air pressure helps to push spectators out the doors.

8   The Metrodome can be used for both amateur and professional sports. These include baseball, football, basketball, volleyball, soccer, and roller blading. It can be converted from a baseball field for the Minnesota Twins to a football field for the Minnesota Vikings in about two hours. Retractable[1] seats—7,600 of them—are stored

---

[1]capable of being folded up out of the way

against the right field wall for baseball and unfolded for football games. The pitcher's mound, which weighs 23,000 pounds, can be lowered three feet by the push of a button.

9   The interior space of the Metrodome, 60 million cubic feet, equals the volume of 3,300 homes. It seats 55,500 for baseball and 63,000 for football.

The Metrodome in Minneapolis

10   Want to rent the Metrodome? You can, for $1,000 an hour. One February, a Minnesota man just couldn't wait for summer, so he rented the Metrodome. He put down sand and wading pools and transformed the arena into a beach.

Checking Comprehension

What are some unusual features of the Metrodome?
What different sports can be played there?

---

11   When the Minnesota Twins and Minnesota Vikings moved to the Metrodome, their old stadium in Bloomington, Minnesota, became vacant. This space was just a few miles from the twin cities of Minneapolis and St. Paul. It was a great location. What could it be used for? Developers came up with all kinds of ideas.

12   The Twin Cities area seemed just the right place for an enclosed mall. Shopping can be an ordeal when the temperature dips below zero. Some of Minnesota's downtown stores and offices have skywalks.[2] Shoppers use these enclosed bridges to get from one building to another. An entire indoor shopping mall would attract customers.

13   Bloomington finally went along with two brothers who could think big. The Ghermezian [Gur·may'zee·un] brothers had created the world's largest mall in Alberta, Canada. Their West Edmonton Mall has more than 700 shops, an amusement park, aquariums, a hockey stadium, a skating rink, a water park, and underwater submarine rides.

14   For Minnesota, the Ghermezians had to scale down their plans a bit. To get financing, they had to team up with other developers and bankers. They also had to cope with hostility from the community. Retailers worried that a megamall would put them out of business. But despite many obstacles, construction of Mall of America began in 1988. It was completed in August 1992, at a cost of $625 million.

15   Located on a 78-acre site, the interior space is 4.2 million square feet! It's as long as four football fields and as wide as three. Each three-level shopping avenue has its own style. West Market is a street scene alive with kiosks [key'ahsks][3] and street vendors. North Garden is a land-

---

[2]enclosed walkways that connect buildings
[3]stands enclosed on three sides

The entrance of Mall of America

scaped park setting. South Boulevard looks like a shopping district in Europe. East Broadway has the bright lights and color of its New York namesake.

16   This gigantic rectangle has four major stores (Sears, Macy's, Nordstrom, and Bloomingdale's), one on each corner. On three floors, about 350 smaller shops line the four corridors of the rectangle. The mall's smaller shops range from the familiar to the extraordinary. While some are high-priced, others are bargain hunters' delights. One shop sells nightshirts decorated with human skeletons. Another store has stuffed animals hanging from tree branches. An athletic store has an archery range, an artificial ski slope, a batting cage, and a boxing ring. Customers can try out equipment before they buy it.

Checking Comprehension
Why is Mall of America referred to as a megamall?
What unusual stores are in the mall?

17   In the center of the mall's rectangle is the largest enclosed theme park in the United States. The 27-acre park has 23 rides and attractions. Knott's Camp Snoopy features rides and games based on Minnesota's waterfalls, lakes, and woods. Visitors see models of Charlie Brown, Snoopy, and the whole "Peanuts" comic strip gang at camp. Workers dress like scouts, with matching shirts, shorts, and scarf ties. This camp honors Charles M. Schulz, born in Minneapolis in 1922 and creator of "Peanuts," the most successful comic strip ever.

Knott's Camp Snoopy in Mall of America

18   Paul Bunyan's Log Ride sends passengers seated in logs zooming down a 40-foot waterfall. They ride through

caves with 13 robotic figures, including Paul Bunyan and his blue ox, Babe. The legendary giant lumberjack[4] once lived and worked in Minnesota. At least, that's what Minnesota residents claim.

19   Wilderness Theater stars wild animals and teaches children about ecology.[5] The Ford Playhouse Theater shows 3-D films. When viewers put on the special dark glasses, butterflies and sharks get too close for comfort. In the Lego Imagination Center, huge dinosaurs built from plastic blocks move and flash their eyes.

20   During the day, the sun shines in through a skylight. Visitors walk on sidewalks. Trees grow here and there. Camp Snoopy feels like the great outdoors. But instead of temperatures below 0, this park's temperature is kept at a steady 70 degrees.

21   Next to Camp Snoopy is Golf Mountain. It's a two-level miniature golf course landscaped with several waterfalls and mountain paths. In the theater complex, moviegoers can choose from 14 films. For fast meals, there are two food courts that seat 1,000 customers each. For more formal dining, the mall has 20 full-service restaurants. Nightclub entertainment includes country music and comedy.

22   In addition, there's Entertrainment. It's a huge, interactive exhibit of model trains running on five different levels. This miniature world goes through a 24-hour cycle of day and night in just 15 minutes.

23   The mall employs 10,000 people, an economic benefit to the community. How will it affect other shopping centers in the area? Only time will tell. But, whether people like the mall or hate it, they must admit it's unique. In a nation of 38,000 shopping centers, Mall of America is the only one that people visit for a vacation.

---

[4]someone employed to cut trees for lumber
[5]the pattern of relationships between living things and their
 environments

24　　During its first six months, Mall of America had 16 million visitors. By 1996, its developers expect 40 million visitors a year. That would top Walt Disney World's figures of 25 to 30 million visitors annually. Mall developers hope to add a walk-through aquarium 300 feet long and a lot more attractions. They'll do this if the crowds keep coming.

Shops inside Mall of America

25　　Because of its many lakes and forests, Minnesota is a popular vacation spot. People have long enjoyed fishing, boating, and hunting there. Now Mall of America attracts people who enjoy an indoor hobby—shopping.

Checking Comprehension

What kinds of entertainment can be found at Mall of America?

Could someone live at the mall without going outside?

Is the mall a place children enjoy?

SIDELIGHTS

About the Twin Cities

Minneapolis and St. Paul are the country's largest twin cities. St. Paul is the capital of Minnesota, and Minneapolis is the state's largest city. About half of the state's 4.2 million people live in this area. The Twin Cities boast two major symphony orchestras and the world-famous Guthrie Theater.

The Minneapolis Sculpture Garden has Claes Oldenberg and Coosje [Koh'shu] van Bruggen's sculpture *Spoonbridge and Cherry*. Its 52-foot spoon holds a 1,200-pound cherry. The spoon spans a pool. The cherry's stem sprays a mist of water.

About Minnesota, the North Star State

- The coldest day: February 9, 1899. It was −59° F in northern Minnesota.
- The longest snowstorm: In December, 1950, Duluth had a snowstorm 118 hours long and 35 inches deep.
- Names and nicknames: *Minni-* means "water"; *sotah* means "sky-tinted" or "clouded." It's the land of sky blue waters. The Land of 10,000 Lakes really has more than 15,000—great for water sports.
- The Paul Bunyan heritage: In Bemidji [Bu·mij'ee], there is a 26-foot wooden statue of Paul Bunyan with a 15-foot Babe.

Making Inferences

Reread the paragraph(s) indicated after each statement.
Then decide if each statement is probably true or false.

_____ 1. Residents of Minnesota cope with winter
weather in many creative ways. (paragraphs 1–5)
_____ 2. The Metrodome is not as large as indoor
stadiums in other parts of the country.
(paragraph 6)
_____ 3. A baseball field is larger than a football field.
(paragraphs 8–9)
_____ 4. It's fairly inexpensive to rent the Metrodome for
a private party. (paragraph 10)
_____ 5. Mall of America offers entertainment for both
children and adults. (paragraphs 15–22)

Practicing Vocabulary

Circle the correct word or phrase to complete each
sentence.

1. Mall of America is (outdoors, circular, unpopular,
enclosed).
2. A stadium that is versatile (has one use, can be used
for many activities, has artificial grass, is enclosed).
3. The grass at the Metrodome is (artificial, crystal,
obvious, unique).
4. People who live in Minnesota are (natives, residents,
artificial, retractable).
5. The Metrodome is (a stadium, an aquarium, a
megamall, a dome).

Talking It Over

1. Sometimes people go to shopping malls even when they don't plan to buy anything. What are some of the reasons?

2. Do you have a favorite work of sculpture? Is it big or small? Do you think sculpture must be large to be important?

3. Have you ever attended a football or baseball game indoors? How does it compare to a game held outdoors? Which do you prefer?

4. Do you like a cold climate or a warm one? What are the advantages or disadvantages of each?

5. What things and events in this reading show that people in Minnesota have a sense of humor?

ANSWER KEY

Making Inferences, page 14
1. True.
2. True.
3. False. It is 2,000 feet above sea level.
4. False. It is too hot to play tennis.
5. True.
6. True.
7. False. The divorce and marriage laws are the same all over Nevada.

Practicing Vocabulary, page 14
1. revenue 2. an oasis 3. ancient 4. A video 5. fighting
6. mirage 7. casinos

Talking It Over, page 15
1. Answers will vary. Some believe that gambling becomes addictive or that poor people, who cannot afford to lose money, take chances to improve their lot. Others think that the revenue from gambling allows states to improve their services in areas such as education and health care.
2. Answers will vary. Some gamblers become compulsive in hopes of winning big or improving their lifestyle. Others enjoy the excitement of taking high-stakes risks.
3. Answers will vary.
4. Although neon signs make Las Vegas more glitzy, the slot machine was probably more important to the success of Las Vegas. Gamblers would come to Las Vegas even without neon signs.

ELVIS'S KINGDOM

Making Inferences, page 30
1. True. His appearances on the Ed Sullivan show especially made him famous.
2. False. He was the performer who made the style popular worldwide.
3. True. He was devoted to his mother. He obeyed the teachings of his religion. He did what his manager told him to do.

4. True. The drugs he took were all prescribed by his doctor. He also went to the White House to offer President Nixon his help in the nation's fight against drug abuse.
5. False. He didn't seek disapproval from adults. He moved in response to the music, out of nervousness, and to be visually entertaining.
6. False. Elvis was generous with others, but he also spent a lot of money on his house, cars, and airplanes.
7. False. It is very lavish and, many say, decorated in bad taste.
8. True. But he did not try to be immoral, and is not immortal.

Practicing Vocabulary, page 30
1. estate 2. immoral 3. fans 4. imitate 5. remember
6. too valuable to set a price on

Talking It Over, page 31
1. Answers will vary. Sometimes a person who was once poor and has become rich craves possessions that display his or her success.
2. Answers will vary.
3. Answers will vary.
4. Elvis had a sense of humor. Elvis also felt some anger and bitterness toward Parker because of his control over Elvis's career and personal life.

ENCHANTED LAND

Making Inferences, page 44
1. False. Here, the word *itch* means a desire for something.
2. True. They came for the clear air and large, unpopulated areas.
3. False. It has a higher percentage of Hispanics, not a higher absolute number.
4. False. New Mexican cuisine includes homegrown products and foods eaten by the pioneers of the American West.
5. False. They lived there by A.D. 1000 (1,000 years ago).
6. True.
7. False. He lived in his own home in Taos.

Practicing Vocabulary, page 44
1. clay and mud 2. pueblos 3. chilis 4. peak 5. diversity

Talking It Over, page 45
1. This reading tells about Indians who lived in villages on Indian land. But today, Native Americans live where they choose, and many do not live on reservations.

2. Santa Fe is unusual because of its adobe architecture, beautiful scenery, appeal to art admirers and artists, and rich cultural offerings, especially in the areas of art, music, and museums that deal with folk cultures.
3. Answers will vary. As the heated air in a hot-air balloon cools, the balloon comes down. The sideways direction cannot be controlled precisely. But a balloonist can control the height and search for a breeze in the direction the balloonist wants to travel. Sometimes it's impossible to get the balloon to a selected spot.
4. Answers will vary. Students may mention various sites included in the Sidelights list, the scenic beauty of the land, or the various ethnic cultures and artifacts that are abundant in New Mexico.
5. Answers will vary. The technology that led to the atomic bomb has also been used for peaceful purposes. New advancements that are used to benefit the Earth and its inhabitants can be termed progress. Those that harm the Earth cannot be labeled as progress.

ALOHA!

Making Inferences, page 60

1. False. Myths are made up to explain events. They are usually not true.
2. True. No one lived on the Hawaiian Islands that long ago.
3. True. Because of the Islands' location, airports were necessary for further development.
4. False. Although there is snow skiing, water sports are more popular by far.
5. False. Missionaries outlawed the hula.
6. True. Part of the monument is the sunken ship just as part of Hawaii is underwater.

Practicing Vocabulary, page 60

1. curious 2. mountain 3. Hulas 4. sacrificed 5. broken
6. salvaged

Talking It Over, page 61

1. People create myths and legends to provide explanations for things they don't understand. They also seem to give credit for the creation of the universe to gods or mythical forces.
2. Answers will vary.

3. Death is often a part of sacrifice, but in ancient and tribal cultures, animals and even people may have been sacrificed against their will. In war, also, not all people who sacrifice their lives for their country choose to do so.
4. Answers will vary.
5. There are still taboos against some practices, such as the marriage of relatives to one another. Other answers are possible.
6. Answers will vary.
7. Answers will vary.

LA LA LAND

Making Inferences, page 74
1. True. That's why the L.A. Chamber of Commerce was raising money to rebuild the *Hollywood* sign.
2. False. The first films were made in New York, Chicago, and New Jersey.
3. True.
4. False. Companies that give tours know their addresses, and tourists can buy books that list them.
5. True. Oscars are also given for outstanding directing, photography, set design, costumes, sound, film editing, etc.
6. False. The traffic congestion often creates long waits.

Practicing Vocabulary, page 74
Part A.
1. cement 2. celebrities 3. curiosity 4. outstanding 5. smog
Part B.
A *country* is the land of a person's birth, heritage, or residence; a *county* is a division of a state. *Weather* refers to conditions for a particular day or period of time; *climate* refers to seasonal patterns. A *visitor* may go to a place to see friends or relatives; a *tourist* is a sightseer, someone who goes to see a place. A *signature* is the written name of a person; an *autograph* is the signature of a famous person given as a souvenir.

Talking It Over, page 75
1. Answers will vary. Some elements of a good movie include an interesting plot with some surprises, good acting, and effective photography. To make a good movie, people with many different talents must work together. It is a collaborative art.
2. Answers will vary.

3. Today, many women consider the term *actress* demeaning. Many women dislike any label that identifies sex when that information is irrelevant. Other words ending in *-ess* that are out of favor now are *authoress*, *Negress*, and *waitress*.
4. Answers will vary. Some fans see stars as heroes they look up to. Other fans wonder if the stars look as glamorous in real life as they do on the screen.
5. Answers will vary.

WINTER WONDERLAND

Making Inferences, page 86
1. True.
2. False. It is the largest indoor multiple-use stadium with an air-supported dome.
3. True. That's why the Metrodome has to retract some seats for baseball games.
4. False. It costs $1,000 per hour to rent the Metrodome.
5. True.

Practicing Vocabulary, page 86
1. enclosed 2. can be used for many activities 3. artificial
4. residents 5. a stadium

Talking It Over, page 87
1. Answers will vary. Malls offer opportunities for people to socialize. They also host art fairs, concerts, demonstrations of merchandise, book-signing parties, and celebrity appearances. Some people spend time at malls just so they are not alone. Crowded malls also attract shoplifters and pickpockets.
2. Answers will vary.
3. Answers will vary. Many people would agree that playing or watching sports indoors is less exciting than outdoors but more comfortable.
4. Answers will vary.
5. Some funny things and activities mentioned in the reading include the races held in International Falls, the Lego dinosaurs, the Camp Snoopy rides, the gigantic sculpture of Paul Bunyan, and *Spoonbridge and Cherry*.